A Taste of culture

Foods of Ghana

Barbara Sheen

KIDHAVEN PRESS
A part of Gale, Cengage Learning

GALE
CENGAGE Learning·

Detroit • New York • San Francisco • New Haven, Conn • Waterville, Maine • London

LIBRARY OF CONGRESS CATALOGING-IN-PUBLICATION DATA

Sheen, Barbara.
  Foods of Ghana / by Barbara Sheen.
    p. cm. -- (A taste of culture)
  Includes bibliographical references and index.
  ISBN 978-0-7377-5949-5 (hardcover)
  1. Cooking, Ghanaian--Juvenile literature. 2. Food--Ghana--Juvenile
literature. 3. Cookbooks--Juvenile literature. 4. Ghana--Social life and
customs--Juvenile literature. I. Title.
  TX725.G4S54 2012
  641.59667--dc23
                                                        2011039891

Kidhaven Press
27500 Drake Rd.
Farmington Hills MI 48331

ISBN-13: 978-0-7377-5949-5
ISBN-10: 0-7377-5949-6

Printed in the United States of America
1 2 3 4 5 6 7 16 15 14 13 12

Contents

Essential Ingredients

Ghana is a small country in West Africa located only a few degrees north of the equator. It is a land of scenic beauty, rich culture, fertile soil, and mineral wealth. Ghanaian cooking depends on fresh ingredients that come from the country's soil and waters. Among the most essential are starchy vegetables and fruit, corn, fish and seafood, and chili peppers. They are a part of almost every meal.

Yams, Cassavas, and Plantains

Starchy foods such as yams, **cassavas**, and **plantains** that taste similar to white-fleshed baking potatoes are

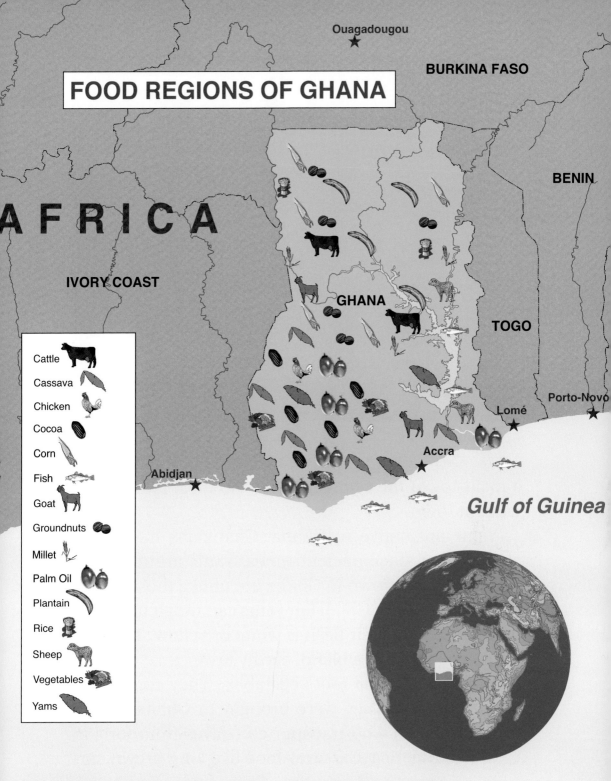

The cassava root is a starchy vegetable that resembles long brown carrots.

a mainstay of the Ghanaian diet. No meal is complete without them.

Yams are native to Ghana. Ghanaians have been eating them since ancient times. Yams are root vegetables. Those grown in Ghana are unlike those grown in North America. Ghanaian yams can weigh up to 100 pounds (45kg). Their flesh is white or yellow. They are not sweet but have a bland, earthy taste.

Cassavas are also root vegetables. They come from South America. They were brought to Ghana by European seamen who transported slaves from forts in Ghana to America. Cassavas look like long brown car-

The Slave Trade

Between 1650 and 1860 about 10–15 million Africans were forced into slavery in North and South America and the Caribbean. Fourteen percent were Ghanaians.

Potential slaves were kidnapped by African traders in exchange for guns and other items from Europe. Captured people were marched long distances to European forts on the west coast of Africa. About half died on the way.

The survivors were transported across the Atlantic Ocean on a three-month journey known as the Middle Passage. Conditions were horrible. Captives were chained to each other and forced to lie on their backs with their heads between the legs of others. About 2 million people died on these voyages.

Upon their arrival in the Americas, the captives were sold as slaves. The ships returned to Europe with goods from the Americas. In Europe, the goods were exchanged for guns bound for Africa.

rots. They are covered by tough skin. Inside, they contain snow-white flesh. Plantains, on the other hand, are a fruit. They look like large green bananas but are too hard and bitter to be eaten raw. First-century Arab traders brought them to Africa from Asia.

Ghanaians boil, bake, fry, and mash these starches. Most importantly, they turn them into **fufu** (foo-foo), a staple food that is eaten like bread. Fufu looks like a ball of freshly kneaded dough. It is made of pounded cassava, plantain, and/or yams, either individually or in combination. It takes two people and lots of muscle and coordination to make fufu. First the cassava, yams, and/or plantains are boiled to soften them. Then they are put in a large wooden bowl, or **mortar,** that stands about 2 feet (0.60m) high. One person pounds the fufu with a long club, or **pestle,** that looks like a small tree trunk with a flat bottom. Another person moves and folds the mixture in between strokes. Canadian journalist Zoe Ackah, who spent a year in Ghana, describes the process: "Thrusting a tree trunk up and down and not breaking the other person's hand is an exercise for people with good rhythm, and this pounding process takes about 25 minutes....The first time I tried it, I ripped some skin off my fingers...and I couldn't lift my arms for three days."[1]

Once the mixture is smooth and elastic, fufu is formed into a ball and soup is poured over it. "The fufu should sit like an island in a sea of soup, with the meat and fish scattered over the top,"[2] explains Ghanaian author Dorinda Hafner.

Ghanaians do not tradi-

Fufu, a bread-like staple food in Ghana, is made by pounding boiled cassava, plantain, or yam, in a bowl with a club.

tionally use utensils. Fufu serves as an edible spoon. Diners break off small pieces with which they scoop up the soup. Fufu is never chewed. Ghanaians just pop it into their mouths and swallow. It is so soft and moist that it slides right down.

Corn

Corn is another important part of the Ghanaian people's diet. Corn arrived in Ghana in the 1600s on slave ships from North America. It thrived in Ghana's rich soil and soon became a popular food.

Ghanaians prefer white corn to yellow corn. It has a harder, drier texture than yellow corn. Ghanaians grill corn, boil it with peanuts, coconuts, or beans, and they grind it into cornmeal. Fermented cornmeal is the main ingredient in kenkey (ken-kay) and banku (bahn-ku), popular cornmeal dumplings. The cornmeal is mixed with water and left in a warm place until harmless bacteria form on it, which gives the cornmeal a tangy sour flavor. The cornmeal is then formed into dough. It looks and smells like the dough used to make sourdough bread. To make banku, Ghanaians cook the dough in water until it forms a smooth, soft paste, which they form into dumplings.

Making kenkey is more complicated. First, the dough is partially cooked in water. Then it is wrapped in corn husks and steamed until it is hot, moist, and tender. Kenkey resembles Latin American tamales when they are done. Both banku and kenkey have a tart flavor and aroma. Banku is usually eaten with soups and stews. Kenkey is topped with fried fish and hot pepper sauce.

A woman makes kenkey by stirring and cooking a pot of cornmeal.

Freshly Caught

Kenkey is not the only food eaten with fish. Ghana borders the Gulf of Guinea, which is part of the Atlantic Ocean. It has 344 miles (550km) of coastline plus many inland waterways, including Lake Volta, the largest man-made lake in the world. Many kinds of water creatures live in Ghana's waters, including shrimp,

Corn and Beans

Corn boiled with beans, fresh coconut, or roasted peanuts is a popular dish in Ghana. Canned, frozen, or fresh corn can be used. White corn is most authentic. A cup of shelled, roasted peanuts or fresh coconut can be substituted for the black-eyed peas.

Ingredients
2 cups corn kernels
1 cup canned black-eyed peas, drained
½ cup water
1 teaspoon red pepper flakes
Salt and pepper to taste

Instructions
1. Combine the corn, beans, and water in a pot and cook over medium heat uncovered until the corn is tender, about 5 minutes.
2. Stir in the red pepper flakes, salt, and pepper.
Serves 2–4.

clams, crabs, sardines, tilapia, anchovies, and tuna. Fish and seafood are an important source of protein in Ghana. Fishing is a part of many Ghanaians' lives. It is usually a communal activity. In coastal villages, fishermen paddling long, colorful, dugout canoes cast giant nets out into the ocean. Other villagers line up on the beach and haul in the nets. It takes lots of people to pull them in. As the nets are dragged onto the beach, women and children grab the still wriggling fish and put them in baskets. The catch is divided among all the

The Gold Coast

Until 1957, Ghana was known as the Gold Coast because of its mineral wealth. Ghana's first contact with Europeans occurred in the 1400s when Portuguese seamen arrived. They encountered different groups of native people, some of whom controlled large underground gold deposits. When news of the area's gold deposits spread, gold seekers from England, Germany, Portugal, the Netherlands, Sweden, and Denmark arrived.

These groups struggled to control the gold deposits. In 1821, the British took control of the country. The Ashanti people, the largest ethnic group, whose empire controlled most of the Gold Coast, resisted. The British and the Ashanti fought four wars. Ultimately, the British won. They ruled the Gold Coast until 1957, when the country gained its independence. It was the first sub-Saharan African nation to become independent. It renamed itself Ghana, after an ancient African empire.

participants. Some of the catch is smoked in clay ovens or sun-dried to preserve it for future use. Some of the fish are taken to markets by women who carry them in baskets perched on their heads. The rest is eaten minutes after it is pulled from the sea.

Ghanaians fry, bake, boil, and grill fish and seafood. They top it with spinach, tomatoes, and onions. They build soups and stews around it. They pour spicy sauce over it. "With so much of Ghana's fresh food gathered from the ocean, I sometimes think Ghanaians should have flippers and fins! Fish is eaten in all possible va-

In the coastal regions of Ghana, fishing is a community activity. Fisherman use long, dugout canoes (shown) or cast nets from the beach.

rieties and combinations in my country,"[3] Hafner explains.

Perfectly Spiced

Chili peppers add zest to fish and seafood dishes. Cooks use the hot peppers to enhance the flavor of almost everything. Chili peppers are used fresh, and they are dried and pounded into fiery red powder. They are also combined with dried shrimp, tomatoes, and onions, then fried in oil to make **shitor** (she-toe), a spicy dark brown sauce that accompanies almost every meal.

Chili peppers are not native to Africa. Fifteenth-century Portuguese seamen coming from South America brought the peppers to Ghana. The Ga (Gah) people,

Shitor

Shitor (she-toe) is not difficult to make. Adding more or less chili powder changes the spiciness.

Ingredients
1¼ cups vegetable oil
1 onion, minced
3 tablespoons red chili powder
1 tablespoon ground ginger
¼ cup dried shrimp, ground
1 tablespoon tomato paste
1 chicken or fish bouillon cube, crushed

Instructions
1. Heat the oil in a pan over medium heat. Add the onions and cook until they are golden.
2. Stir in the tomato paste.
3. Mix together the remaining ingredients and add them to the pan. Stir continuously until the mixture darkens, about 3 minutes. Let the shitor cool for about an hour before serving.

Serves 2–4.

Red chili peppers are a main ingredient in shitor.

one of Ghana's many tribal groups, were the first to make shitor. Today, almost every cook has his or her own special recipe. Some add ginger, garlic, and/or soup flavoring cubes. Some make it blisteringly hot, while others prefer it mild. The sauce has a strong, salty taste and a pungent aroma. It can be stored for a year without spoiling. Many secondary-school-aged children in Ghana attend boarding school. Most take a jar of their mother's shitor with them. "It goes with just about anything—fried yam or potato, hardboiled eggs, samosas, spring rolls, fried fish, meat, beans, etc.— anything you like spicy,"[4] explains Ghanaian blogger Eunice Ekor.

Ghanaians do like their food spicy, but not so spicy that the heat of the peppers overpowers the taste of the other ingredients. "Everything," says Travel Channel host Anthony Bourdain, "is fresh. Everything is spicy, but not too spicy. Every meal is delicious."[5] Essential ingredients like cassava, plantains, yams, fish and seafood, corn, and chili peppers help to make it so.

chapter

2

It Takes a Full Stomach to Blow a Horn

An old Ghanaian proverb says: "It takes a full stomach to blow a horn."[6] Ghanaians work hard. Many villages lack modern conveniences, and physical labor is a way of life for villagers. Hearty meals give Ghanaians the energy they need. In fact, Ghanaians do not feel like they have truly eaten unless they have a heavy meal. Soups, stews, and sauces accompanied by starches fit the bill. They are Ghanaians' favorite dishes and the mainstay of Ghanaian cooking.

Favorite Soups

Soup poured over fufu is a common Ghanaian meal. Although Ghanaian soups start with water, they are

About Ghana

Ghana is a developing nation in West Africa. It is about the size of the state of Oregon with a population of about 22 million. It is bordered by Togo, Cote de Ivoire (the Ivory Coast), Burkina Faso, and the Gulf of Guinea. It has a hot tropical climate, which is rainy in the summer and dry in the winter. Within its borders are coastal plains, rain forests, savannas, and mountains. Lake Volta, Ghana's largest lake, is two-thirds the length of the country.

The capital is Accra. Kumasi and Tamale are other major cities. The official language is English, but there are more than fifty local languages.

Ghana has the longest history of democratic elections in Africa. It is a republic. The president is elected every four years.

The country is rich in such natural resources as gold, diamonds, oil, hydroelectricity, bauxite, and manganese. Its currency is the cedi (seedy).

thicker and heartier than North American soups. Cooks thicken them with nuts, seeds, or beans.

Ghanaians make a wide variety of soups. **Groundnut** soup is among the most popular. Ghanaians call peanuts groundnuts because they grow close to the ground. To make the soup, cooks pound fresh peanuts into a paste much like unsweetened peanut butter. Then they cook the paste in water. What else goes in the soup depends on the cook. In Ghana, recipes are not usually written down. Cooking instructions are loose,

Groundnut soup, like this one made of peanuts, tomatoes and lamb, is a popular dish in Ghana.

and cooking times and measurements are rarely given. Ghanaians prefer to be creative. They change proportions and ingredients depending on their budget, what vegetables are freshest, and their personal taste. Hafner explains: "I have had enormous problems trying to translate my typically African 'let's estimate' style of cooking into easy-to-follow, easy-to-identify Western recipes. My mother and her mother before her have always cooked straight from their hearts, and this is the way I cook, too."[7]

Usually, groundnut soup contains peanut paste, onions, tomatoes, chili peppers, and chicken. Since many Ghanaians do not own gas or electric stoves, cooking is usually done outdoors on a **brazier,** or coal pot, a simple cooking device consisting of a container of live coals covered by a thin metal top that heats one pot at a time. The soup is cooked slowly and stirred often by

Groundnut Soup

This is an easy way to make groundnut soup. It uses already cooked chicken to make preparation faster. Add more or less crushed red pepper to taste. It can be eaten as soup or served over rice.

Ingredients
4 cups chicken broth
1–2 cups cooked chicken, cut into small pieces
1 onion, chopped
3 large tomatoes, chopped
1 cooked sweet potato, skin removed, mashed
1 teaspoon crushed red pepper flakes
½ teaspoon ground ginger
¾ cup creamy peanut butter

Instructions
1. Put tomatoes, onion, ginger, and red pepper flakes in a blender and puree.
2. Combine the sweet potato, broth, and puree. Cook on medium until the soup boils.
3. Reduce the heat to low. Add the peanut butter. Cook until the soup thickens, stirring often.
Serves 4.

the cook, who sits on the ground beside the brazier. The result is a thick, creamy soup with a nutty, spicy taste. A few spoonfuls poured over fufu is incredibly filling.

Light soup is another favorite. Its name refers not to its heartiness, but rather to its color. Light soup is a peppery soup of countless variations. Commonly, it is made with chicken, lamb, or beef; tomatoes; onions; chili peppers; dried chili flakes; and white, egg-sized eggplant, or garden eggs as they are known in Ghana. It is thickened with ground white beans or ground watermelon seeds. To use watermelon seeds, cooks first remove the bitter black outer shell of the seeds, leaving behind the soft white interior that looks and tastes like pumpkin seeds. Customarily, light soup is quite spicy. Most diners are not satisfied unless the soup makes their noses run and brings tears to their eyes.

Stews

Like soup, stews of all kinds are widely eaten. Ghanaian soups and stews have a lot in common, but they differ in two ways. Stews are thicker than soups, and they are prepared differently. All the ingredients in soups are cooked by boiling. The main ingredients in Ghanaian stews, however, are fried in plenty of oil before water or broth is added. Groundnut stew, for instance, is very similar to groundnut

soup except the stew is denser, oilier, and infinitely richer. A bowl of Ghanaian stew, according to Bourdain, "is a meal...enough food for a whole day...perfect, spicy, hearty."[8]

There are hundreds of varieties of Ghanaian stews. All are incredibly filling. Okra stew is a favorite. Okra is native to Africa and is very popular throughout the

Okra is native to Ghana, and is used extensively in stews.

continent. Ghanaians enjoy its slippery, gooey texture. Author Jessica Harris explains: "The slime…is actually thought to be a virtue [positive quality]. Cutting the pod increases okra's 'sticking power' and some recipes from western Africa call for the pod to be minced into a gluey mass."[9]

To make the stew, cooks cut okra into tiny gooey rounds, which they fry with onions, tomatoes, and chili peppers. Water is added and the mixture is slowly cooked with eggplant, dried shrimp, salted fish, and ham. The variety of flavors, textures, and aromas produces a full-bodied dish with a smoky, earthy taste and scent. It is served with rice, boiled yams or cassava, or banku.

Jollof (jull-of) rice is another specialty. It originated with the Wolof people of Senegal and Gambia and spread to Ghana. It is similar to jambalaya, a rice dish from Louisiana. In fact, many dishes that are popular in the southern part of the United States have their roots in dishes that slaves from West Africa brought to America.

Jollof rice is a tomato-based stew. It is made with rice, tomatoes, red chili peppers, onions, curry powder, nutmeg, and soup flavoring cubes. It is known for its vibrant red color, which comes from the tomatoes and peppers. To make it, cooks fry the tomatoes, peppers, onions, and spices. Then they add the water and rice. The whole thing is left to cook until the rice absorbs all the liquid and is coated with the tomato mixture.

Jollof rice, pictured here with fried chicken and fried plantains, is a popular dish across West Africa.

Businesswomen

Ghana has many outdoor markets where fresh fruit and vegetables are sold. Women known as produce queens run the markets. Each queen is a vendor elected by her peers to act as an intermediary between farmers and vendors of a certain type of fruit or vegetable. For instance, the tomato queen works with all the farmers and vendors of vegetables with seeds such as tomatoes, eggplants, chilies, and okra. Yam queens deal with yams and potatoes, and plantain queens deal with plantains and bananas. The queens settle disputes between farmers who bring produce to the market and the vendors they sell their produce to. They inspect the produce to make sure it is fresh and unblemished. They negotiate bulk buying prices, set market prices, and supervise laborers who move the produce through the market. The queens are well-respected. Their decisions are rarely questioned.

The red fluffy rice is topped with fried chicken or fish. It is often served with salad and fried plantains. It is, according to Kajal "Kate" Tejsinghani, a blogger, cook, and world traveler, "a very flavorful and aromatic one pot rice meal."[10]

Sauces or Gravies

Sauces, or **"gravies,"** as they are called in Ghana, are other hearty favorites. Unlike stews and soups, sauces do not contain water and they are not boiled. They are fried in lots of oil and typically contain four basic ingredients—tomatoes, onions, chili peppers, and

Red-Red

In Ghana, red-red is made with red palm oil. This recipe uses vegetable oil, which is easier to find. Red-red is good served over rice.

Ingredients

2 15-oz. cans black-eyed peas, drained
¼ cup vegetable oil
1 15-oz. can crushed or diced tomatoes
1 onion, sliced
3 garlic cloves, sliced
1 teaspoon ginger
1 chili pepper, sliced
salt and pepper to taste

Instructions

1. Heat the oil in a large saucepan. Add the onion, chili pepper, and garlic. Cook over medium heat until the onions are clear.
2. Add the black-eyed peas, tomatoes, ginger, salt ,and pepper. Cook on low about 10 minutes, stirring often.

Serves 4 as a main dish or 6–8 as a side dish.

A favorite dish, red-red, is made with cow peas, or black-eyed peas.

dried shrimp or **crayfish,** to which bits of cooked meat, chicken, fish, seafood, and/or vegetables are added. The proportions of the basic ingredients and the additional ingredients change the taste and the variety of the sauce.

Palm oil is a red oil that is extracted from palm nuts, the fruit of the oil palm tree. Palm oil gives the popular dish red-red it's distinct red coloring.

Red-red is a popular sauce. It features cow peas, the Ghanaian name for black-eyed peas, cooked in sauce made from the basic ingredients, until the peas are meltingly soft. The dish gets its name from its bright red color, which comes from the **palm oil** it is fried in. Palm oil is red oil that is extracted from palm nuts, the fruit of an African oil palm tree. It is loaded with vitamin A and has a strong, fruity flavor. Traditionally, Ghanaians use so much oil to make red-red that the oil forms a bright red ring around the peas. Red-red tastes similar to chili beans: spicy, hearty, and delicious. It is usually accompanied by fried plantains and is often topped with fried fish.

Palaver (p' lava) sauce is another favorite. This green sauce contains silver beet leaves, a wild green similar to spinach. Many different varieties of wild greens grow in Ghana. Ghanaians eat at least forty different types. Melon seeds, fresh and smoked fish, and bits of beef are also added to the basic sauce. In Ghana, *palaver* means trouble. No one knows why the sauce got this name. It may be because the ingredients are so varied that cooks thought they might not go well together. But that is not the case. As palaver cooks, the different flavors mix and mingle to create a zesty, somewhat slippery-textured sauce that satisfies even the biggest of appetites.

Diners rarely walk away hungry after eating palaver or any popular Ghanaian sauce, stew, or soup. These favorite dishes provide Ghanaians with the kind of fresh, filling, and delicious meals they love.

Tasty Treats

Africans like to snack and Ghanaians are no exception. According to author Jessica Harris, "People walk through the streets of the African continent with their hands full and their mouths moving. They may be nibbling on a simple ear of grilled corn or working their way through a paper roll filled with almonds or melon seeds, but nibblers they are."[11]

Plenty of Choices

Ghanaians have almost unlimited opportunities to snack. Vendors in informal eateries known as chop bars, in little stalls, pushing carts, or carrying pre-cooked food in boxes and baskets on their heads can be found almost everywhere—in outdoor markets, on

Cocoa

Ghana is the world's second-largest producer of cocoa, the beans from which chocolate is made. Cocoa originated in South America. It was introduced to Africa by Portuguese seamen.

Ghanaian farmers started growing cocoa in the mid-19th century. Harvesting the beans involves gathering and splitting open the large golden pods that hold the beans. The beans are scooped out and covered with banana leaves. They are left to dry and ferment for about six days. This enhances the flavor of the chocolate. The beans are sold to processors in Europe who turn the beans into chocolate candy.

Ghanaian cocoa is considered to be some of the finest in the world. Cocoa production is so important to the nation that the government established a cocoa board and a cocoa research institute to help farmers. Interestingly, because the beans are not processed locally, Ghanaians do not eat a lot of chocolate.

Cocoa beans drying in the sun.

Vendors in Ghanaian markets sell all kinds of snacks, such as bags of popcorn.

city streets, at busy intersections, in bus stations, along roadsides, at sporting events, and on beaches. Explains journalist Lydia Polgreen:

> "Few countries reward the sidewalk chowhound as well as Ghana. From rough-hewn sheds, women sell sharp wedges of starchy yam, perfectly fried... From stainless steel bowls perched atop their heads, women dish out hearty bowls of perfectly spiced stew .... There were fritters made of plantain just this side of too ripe... There were balls of fried dough spiced with a bit of nutmeg, crunchy on the outside and tender on the inside."[12]

Sizzling Grilled Meat

Ghanaians can choose from sweet, savory, hot, cold, solid, or liquid snacks. Kyinkyinga (chi-Cheen-ga) or kebabs are very popular. Kebabs are chunks of meat flavored with spices that are threaded through small, thin wooden skewers and grilled over hot coals. They originated in the Middle East and were brought to Ghana by 13th-century Arab traders. Long before that time, however, Ghanaian tribal people wrapped strips of meat around tall poles. The poles were stuck into the ground, and a fire was built beside them.

Kyinkyinga can be made with any kind of meat. Beef and goat are favorite choices. Before the meat is cooked, it is coated with a mixture of crushed peanuts, cornmeal, chili powder, ginger, and other spices. Some vendors cook the meat on small grills right in front of the customers. Others make the kebabs in advance, wrap them in plastic wrap to keep them warm, and carry them in a small glass cabinet on their heads. According to Hafner, "The vendors rush into traffic stopped at red lights or up to buses and trucks parked at rest stops to try to make a quick sale. The [skill] involved in balancing a heavy glass case full of hot kyinkyinga while simultaneously counting change from a money belt defies description!"[13]

Whether precooked or cooked on the spot, kyinkyinga tastes yummy. The peanut coating seals in the meat's natural juices, resulting in a dish that is crunchy, spicy, and sweetly nutty on the outside and moist and tender within.

Ghanaian People

More than fifty distinct groups make up the Ghanaian people. Almost half of all Ghanaians are Akan people. This ethnic group arrived in Ghana in the 11th century. They speak Twi (Chwee), which is considered to be Ghana's unofficial second language. The Akan people include the Ashanti, Fante, Akyem, and Akuapim tribes. Non-Akan groups include the Ga, Ewe, Gonja, and Mole people.

Of these groups, the Ashanti people were the most powerful in the past. Their king was said to have a golden stool that came from heaven, which he used to unite different Ashanti groups into one state in the 17th century. It covered most of what is now Ghana, Togo, and Cote d'Ivoire and was the largest kingdom in West Africa. The Ashanti empire was rich. It gained its wealth through war and by trading in gold and slaves.

Fresh Treats

Snacks that feature corn, plantains, nuts, or fruit are other favorites. Corn on the cob is very popular. Vendors seated on the side of the road beside charcoal grills sell ears of corn to hungry passers-by. Ghanaians do not rub the corn with butter. Instead, they like to eat it plain accompanied by chunks of fresh coconut.

Peanuts, roasted in hot sand, or melon seeds wrapped in paper cones are other popular natural snacks. So are spicy fried plantains or kelewele (kill-lee-will-lee). To make kelewele, vendors roll plantain chunks in a zesty spice mix made of ginger, chili powder, garlic, and salt. They fry the chunks in hot bubbling oil until the sugar inside the plantain **caramelizes** and the chunks are golden brown. "You got to have hot oil, that is No. 1,"explains Rosemary Nutsungah, a Ghanaian kelewele vendor. "Then the plantain, it can't be too soft. It will drink the oil and become too oily. Also, you have to have very fresh ginger so it be sweet."[14]

The hot chunks are wrapped in newspaper, which absorbs excess oil. They are eaten like French fries while they are soft and hot. They taste slightly sweet, slightly spicy, and absolutely delicious.

Mangos, sweet and juicy tropical fruits, are other natural treats. During January through May, Ghana-

A popular snack in Ghana is kelewele, or fried plantains. They are eaten like french fries while still hot.

Kelewele

Plantains are sold in most supermarkets. Use a knife to remove the peel.

Ingredients
1 large plantain, peeled
4 tablespoons vegetable oil
1 teaspoon chili powder
1 teaspoon ginger
1 teaspoon garlic powder
½ teaspoon salt

Instructions
1. Cut the plantain into half-inch-thick pieces.
2. Mix together 2 tablespoons oil with the spices. Put the plantains in a bowl and pour the spice mix over the plantains. Cover the bowl with foil and refrigerate for one hour.
3. Heat remaining 2 tablespoons of oil in a pan over medium heat. Add the plantains and fry until both sides are golden brown. Drain the oil off the plantains on a paper towel.
Serves 2.

Kelewele is made with fried plantains.

ian mango season, they are a popular dessert as well as a favorite snack. Many different varieties of mangos grow in Ghana. In fact, mango farming is an important industry there. Ghanaian mangos can be small or as large as a coconut. The outer skin can be red, yellow, or green. The inner flesh is a vibrant orange-yellow. During mango season, vendors can be seen almost everywhere sitting and standing behind tall colorful stacks of mangos, which they artfully cut for snackers.

Liquid Refreshments

Vendors offer Ghanaians a wide variety of natural hot and cold drinks, too. Hot drinks, no matter the type, are referred to as tea. Favorite "teas," or hot drinks, include coffee and black and herbal tea, which Ghanaians take with milk and sugar. **Lemongrass** tea is a favorite. Lemongrass is a type of grass with a bulb-shaped base. It has a fresh, light, lemony scent and flavor. Many Ghanaians grow it in their gardens just for tea. They brew the leaves to make a refreshing drink. Since many Ghanaian homes lack refrigerators, Ghanaians often use **evaporated milk** instead of fresh milk in their tea. Evaporated milk is sold in cans. Most of the moisture has been removed from evaporated milk, which keeps it from spoiling. Hibiscus tea is another favorite drink. It is made from the dried petals of hibiscus flowers. The tea is a lovely shade of red, smells like a garden, and tastes pleasingly sweet. It is drunk hot or iced.

Many other cold drinks are sold on Ghanaian streets, too. Some of the drink vendors are children. Cold

Coconut juice is a favorite drink and does not require a special container.

drinks are contained in frozen plastic bags. Ghanaians tear a hole in the corner of the bag, and suck the liquid out while squeezing the bag. Journalist and world traveler Mark Moxon explains:

> "Once you've got the knack, it's wonderfully easy to drink. The first time you try it, things are guaranteed to go wrong, but practice makes perfect....The most popular way to drink from a bag is to nip a hole in one corner....Biting a small hole allows you to squeeze the drink out into your mouth, but the secret isn't just to suck or to squeeze, it's to suck and squeeze; if you just squeeze then the chances are your drink will spill down

the bag and all over your shirt, and if you just suck then the bag collapses and you can't suck anymore…. [In Ghana] even water is sold in bags.…Everywhere you look there are Ghanaians suckling on corners of these little bags."[15]

Drinkable yogurt is also sold in this way. So are fruit squashes, which are fruit drinks made like lemonade with fruit juice, water or club soda, and sugar. Lemon squash, lime squash, and orange squash are favorites. Fresh-squeezed fruit juices are also available almost everywhere. Coconut water and orange juice do not require special containers. Vendors simply cut off the

Lime Squash

Here is a refreshing drink. Water can be substituted for club soda. Honey can be substituted for sugar.

Ingredients
½ cup fresh lime juice
1½ cups cold club soda
4 tablespoons sugar
ice cubes

Instructions
1. Combine all the ingredients in a pitcher. Stir well until the sugar is dissolved.
2. Put ice cubes in 2 glasses. Pour in the lime squash.
Serves 2.

tops of coconuts and oranges. Thirsty Ghanaians tip the coconut and drink out the sweet water or squeeze the orange and suck the juice out.

With cold fresh juices and squashes, hot teas, spicy kebabs, fresh corn on the cob, hot roasted peanuts, delicious fried plantains, and sweet mangos sold almost everywhere, snacking is a way of life in Ghana. Ghanaian street food, according to Bourdain, "Smells good, tastes good, and is amazingly fresh."[16] It is no wonder that stopping for a snack is hard to resist.

Festive Foods

Ghanaians are some of the friendliest and most hospitable people in the world. Sharing food with friends, family, and even with strangers, who soon become friends, is a way of life in Ghana. "You are invited," is heard on buses, in offices, in parks, at sporting events, and in elegant restaurants. It is what diners say to anyone who approaches them. Ghanaians willingly share their food with each other and with tourists, too. It is the way they expect people to behave. "Social interaction, communality, and friendship are fundamental principles guiding Ghanaian lives," explains author Ian Utley.... "Ghanaians will open their arms in friendship to other human beings, in the knowledge that such a gesture will be reciprocated [returned]."[17]   Holidays, festivals, and special occasions give Ghanaians ample opportunities to socialize and share with others.

Many Festivals

Ghanaians like to have fun. Throughout the year, they hold lots of festivals, highlighted by music, dancing, and special foods. One of the biggest is the Homowo (Ho-mo-oo) Festival, which is held in August. The festi-

During the Homowo (hunger go away) festival, priests sprinkle cornmeal down the streets to chase hunger away.

Ghanaian Values

Cooperation, peace, hard work, and being part of a community are important Ghanaian values. Many villages function like extended families with neighbors working together on communal projects and looking out for each other. The elderly are especially respected. They are sought out for advice. They are cared for by their family or neighbors when they are unable to care for themselves. Villagers also help care for each other's children and have no problem reprimanding children when they misbehave. Children are expected to be obedient and respectful to their elders. They are expected to work hard and help around the house.

Tribal loyalty is also valued. Tribal members help each other whenever they can. Family life is very important, too. Family groups that include cousins, uncles, aunts, grandparents, and in-laws get together often. They share food and money.

val honors a time when the Ga people were stricken by **famine**. According to legend, there was a drought that caused their crops to fail. Despite their hunger, the Ga worked hard to get enough food to survive by fishing. They were rewarded by a large fish harvest, which kept them alive until their crops once again thrived. Ghanaians hold the festival to honor the importance of hard work, give thanks for their blessings, and to laugh at hunger. In fact, the term *homowo* means "hunger go away" in Ga.

During the festival, Ghanaians parade through the

streets, sprinkling kpokpoi (poo-poi), bright yellow cornmeal, all over while shouting "homowo." The cornmeal is supposed to chase hunger away. Since there are so many food vendors lining the streets, it is almost impossible to be hungry. Celebrants sing, dance, and eat. "It is a time of joy, of plenty, of singing and dancing in the streets, and of eating until you're so full you can't move,"[18] says Hafner.

Among the many foods associated with the festival is bright red palm nut soup with fish. Its vivid color represents the joy of the celebration, and the fish reminds festivalgoers of the harvest that saved Ghanaians long ago. The soup is made from the pulp of boiled and pounded palm nuts. It is cooked with tomatoes, onions, chili peppers, spices, crab meat, and an assortment of fresh, dried, and salted fish. The soup looks beautiful and tastes and smells wonderful. It has, according to author Fran Osseo-Asare, "a color like paprika or glowing coals, with the softness of red velvet, the silkiness of a fine sari [dress], and the richness of fresh cream."[19]

Oto

Celebrations marking special events in people's lives are another important part of Ghanaian culture. "We celebrate many, many rites of passage," Hafner explains. "The naming of a newborn baby, the purification of a mother after a baby's birth, showing the baby the way to the father's house, the birth of the third boy or girl in a family, puberty rituals, marriage, birthdays,

Ghanaian Homes

Houses in Ghana vary widely. Author Ian Utely provides this description of Ghanaian homes:

It is impossible to describe a "typical" house. The proverbial mud huts are numerous in the villages. Some have wattle [woven branches and twigs]...walls propped up with sticks and leaf roofs. Other people can afford to use sun-dried mud bricks and corrugated iron. In the cities, certain areas are notorious for their slums. At the other end of the scale, you can see some magnificent, three-story mansions with ten or more bedrooms, a swimming pool, and all the modern conveniences. One family will go to the river for their water and the forest for their firewood, while another will simply turn on the hot and cold taps and cook in the microwave or gas oven.

Ian Utley, *Culture Smart!* Ghana. London, England: Kuperard, 2009.

A traditional mud and thatch homestead in Nakpanduri, Ghana.

Birthdays are celebrated with special breakfast foods, such as mashed yams with eggs.

recovery from illness, escaping accidents—the list goes on and on."[20] **Oto** (oh-toe), a bright orange dish consisting of mashed yam mixed with onions and palm oil and topped with chunks of hard-boiled egg, is shared at many of these events, especially birthdays. In the past, when food was sometimes scarce, being served a hard-boiled egg was a luxury reserved for special occasions. Sharing it made the event extra special. Oto remains a traditional birthday breakfast. According to Erin McDonnell, a blogger who lived in Ghana, "You are expected to make a large bowl of oto and then invite your family, neighbors or friends to come and join you in the morning for your birthday breakfast."[21]

Oto is eaten for breakfast on the morning of a wed-

Bananas Ghana

This would taste great with a scoop of vanilla ice cream.

Ingredients
4 bananas, peeled and cut in half lengthwise, and then in half horizontally
¾ cup orange juice
1 teaspoon cinnamon
2 tablespoons sugar
4 teaspoons crushed peanuts

Instructions
1. Preheat the oven to 350° F.
2. Spray a baking dish with nonstick spray.
3. Combine the sugar and cinnamon.
4. Put the bananas in the baking dish. Sprinkle the sugar mix on the bananas. Pour the juice on top.
5. Bake for about 20 minutes. Every few minutes baste the bananas with the juice.

Top with crushed peanuts. Serve warm or at room temperature. Serves 4.

Bananas make this sweet dessert delicious.

ding by a bride and her bridal party, too. "Last month," recalls McDonnell, "while attending the wedding of a woman I have known for eight years, all of us who were at her house helping her get ready, from the hair stylist to the make-up technician on down, all took a small bowl of oto to start the day."[22] The dish not only gives the bride and her friends energy to face the day ahead—it has symbolic meaning. The perfect shape of the egg represents female beauty, while both eggs and yams represent fertility in Ghana.

Sweet Bites

Sweet desserts, too, are often part of special celebrations. Ghanaians do not usually eat elaborate, sugary desserts on a daily basis. They prefer to end their meals with a piece of fresh fruit. However, special treats, which feature fruit, help make special occasions more memorable. Bananas Ghana is especially yummy. It is made by rolling a banana cut into quarters in a mixture of cinnamon and sugar, topping it with orange juice or apricot brandy, an alcoholic beverage, and baking the whole thing until the liquid turns into sticky syrup. The sweet treat is topped with chopped peanuts. It tastes salty, sweet, and tropical. So does peanut and banana cake, another Ghanaian specialty.

Fruit salads are other favorites. Ghana's tropical climate produces an abundance of different fruits. Cutting them up and mixing them together to make a delicious fruit salad is a cooking technique Gha-

Ghanaians often use tropical fruits, such as pineapples, in their fruit salads.

Pineapple Fool

This is a quick and easy dessert. Fresh or canned pineapple can be used.

Ingredients
2 cups chilled, finely chopped pineapple, (drained)
1 cup non-dairy whipped topping
1 teaspoon vanilla
4 teaspoons crushed peanuts

Instructions
1. Mix the whipped topping and vanilla together.
2. Right before serving, mix in the pineapple.
3. Divide the mixture between four parfait glasses or dessert bowls. Top each with a teaspoon of chopped peanuts.
Serves 4.

naians learned from the British who ruled Ghana for more than 100 years. What makes a Ghanaian fruit salad different from most western fruit salads is that some of the fruit is lightly cooked, then cooled before the fruit is added to the salad. Fruit fools are other British contributions. A fool is a creamy mixture of crushed fruit and whipped cream or custard, a sweet similar to vanilla pudding. Ghanaian fools feature tropical fruits like mangos or pineapple. Fools and fruit salads are fresh and cool counterbalances to spicy main dishes.

Twisted Cookies

Atwemo (a-twi-moo), or twisted cookies, is another sweet that is often part of celebrations. The cookies are sold by street vendors and in packages in grocery stores. They are popular at birthday parties and during Christmas. Most Ghanaians are Christians, so Christmas is a festive time in Ghana. It is a time when families and friends visit each other. Twisted cookies are usually kept on hand to welcome visitors.

The cookies get their name from their shape. An oven is not needed to make them. Instead they are fried, which makes them easy to make for those Ghanaians who do not own an oven. The cookies are made from dough that is flavored with sugar, nutmeg, and vanilla, which gives them a warm, mildly sweet flavor and a mouth-watering aroma. Shaping the dough takes skill. First, the cook cuts the dough into little diamonds, which are slit in the middle. Then, the cook pulls one end of the diamond all the way through the slit. This gives the cookies their twisted appearance.

The cookies are fried in hot oil until they are golden. They are left to cool before they are served. They are as crisp as crackers. It is hard to eat just one. That is not a problem because hosts always have plenty to go around. "You're not allowed to leave a Ghanaian's home without a full belly,"[23] Utley explains.

Sharing food is an important part of Ghanaian culture. As a Ghanaian proverb says, "A meal to which one is invited is a delicious meal."[24] Holidays, festivals, and special occasions give Ghanaians many opportunities to share "a delicious meal." Special foods like oto, twisted cookies, fruit desserts, and palm nut soup are vital parts of the fun.

Metric conversions

Mass (weight)

1 ounce (oz.)	= 28.0 grams (g)
8 ounces	= 227.0 grams
1 pound (lb.) or 16 ounces	= 0.45 kilograms (kg)
2.2 pounds	= 1.0 kilogram

Liquid Volume

1 teaspoon (tsp.)	= 5.0 milliliters (ml)
1 tablespoon (tbsp.)	= 15.0 milliliters
1 fluid ounce (oz.)	= 30.0 milliliters
1 cup (c.)	= 240 milliliters
1 pint (pt.)	= 480 milliliters
1 quart (qt.)	= 0.96 liters (l)
1 gallon (gal.)	= 3.84 liters

Pan Sizes

8-inch cake pan	= 20 x 4-centimeter cake pan
9-inch cake pan	= 23 x 3.5-centimeter cake pan
11 x 7-inch baking pan	= 28 x 18-centimeter baking pan
13 x 9-inch baking pan	= 32.5 x 23-centimeter baking pan
9 x 5-inch loaf pan	= 23 x 13-centimeter loaf pan
2-quart casserole	= 2-liter casserole

Temperature

212°F	= 100°C (boiling point of water)
225°F	= 110°C
250°F	= 120°C
275°F	= 135°C
300°F	= 150°C
325°F	= 160°C
350°F	= 180°C
375°F	= 190°C
400°F	= 200°C

Length

1/4 inch (in.)	= 0.6 centimeters (cm)
1/2 inch	= 1.25 centimeters
1 inch	= 2.5 centimeters

Notes

Chapter 1: Essential Ingredients

1. Zoe Ackah. "West African Journal Cooking in Ghana." The Epoch Times, March 14, 2008. http://www.theepochtimes.com/news/8-3-14/67492.html.

2. Dorinda Hafner. *A Taste of Africa.* Berkeley, California: Ten Speed Press, 2002. p. 8.

3. Hafner. *A Taste of Africa,* p. 24.

4. Eunice Ekor. "My Recipe for Shitor." *Cooking in Ghana,* September 14, 2006, http://goodcook.blogspot.com/.

5. Anthony Bourdain. *No Reservations: Ghana.* The Travel Channel, 2007.

Chapter 2: It Takes a Full Stomach to Blow a Horn

6. Quoted in Fran Osseo-Asare. "We Eat First With Our Eyes: On Ghanaian Cuisine." *Betumi.* http://www.betumi.com/home/gastro-fulltext.html#_edn23.

7. Hafner. *A Taste of Africa,* p. 5.

8. Bourdain. *No Reservations: Ghana.*

9. Jessica B. Harris. *The Africa Cookbook.* New York: Simon & Schuster, 1998. p. 65.

10. Kajal Tejsinghani. "Ghanaian Jollof Rice & Beef Kebab." *Aapplemint,* January 27, 2009. http://aapplemint.com/2009/01/27/ghanaian-joll-of-rice-beef-kebab/.

Chapter 3: Tasty Treats

11. Harris. *The Africa Cookbook,* p. 81.

12. Lydia Polgreen. "A Taste of Ghana." *The New York Times*, February 1, 2006. http://www.nytimes.com/2006/02/01/dining/01ghana.html.

13. Hafner. *A Taste of Africa,* p. 54.

14. Quoted in Polgreen. "A Taste of Ghana."

15. Mark Moxon. "Ghana: Drink in a Bag." Mark Moxon's Travel Writing. www.moxon.net/ghana/drink_in_a_bag.html.

16. Bourdain. *No Reservations: Ghana.*

Chapter 4: Festive Foods

17. Ian Utley. *Culture Smart! Ghana.* London, England: Kuperard, 2009, p. 72 -73.

18. Dorinda Hafner. *I Was Never Here and This Never Happened.* Berkeley, California: Ten Speed Press, 1996. p. 64.

19. Osseo-Asare. "We Eat First With Our Eyes: On Ghanaian Cuisine."

20. Hafner. *I Was Never Here and This Never Happened,* p. 5.

21. Erin McDonnell. "Ghanaian Oto: The Breakfast of Brides and Birthday Girls." *The Skinny Gourmet*, February 23, 2008. http://skinnygourmet.blogspot.com/2008/02/ghanaian-oto-breakfast-of-brides-and.html.

22. McDonnell. "Ghanaian Oto: The Breakfast of Brides and Birthday Girls."

23. Utley. *Culture Smart! Ghana,* p. 87.

24. Utley. *Culture Smart! Ghana,* p. 87.

Glossary

brazier: A cooking device consisting of a container of live coals covered by a thin metal top.

caramelizes: A cooking process in which sugar is heated until it dissolves and turns golden brown.

cassava: An edible root plant with a thick skin and white flesh. It is also called yuca and manioc.

crayfish: A shellfish that resembles a small lobster.

evaporated milk: Milk in which most of the moisture has been removed, which keeps it from spoiling.

famine: An extreme scarcity of food.

fufu: A starchy dish made from mashed yams, plantains, and/or cassavas.

gravies: Ghanaian term for any types of sauce.

groundnut: Ghanaian term for a peanut.

lemongrass: A type of grass that has a fresh, light, lemony scent and flavor.

mortar: A bowl-like vessel in which food is mashed or crushed.

oto: A dish, consisting of mashed yam and hard-boiled egg, served on important occasions.

palm oil: Red oil that is extracted from palm nuts, the fruit of an African oil palm tree.

pestle: A bat-shaped tool used to crush or mash food in a mortar.

plantains: Green fruit, resembling bananas, that are eaten cooked.

shitor: A spicy dark brown sauce that accompanies almost every meal in Ghana.

For Further Exploration

Books

Ettagale Blauer, Jason Laure. *Ghana.* New York: Children's Press, 2009. Looks at Ghana's geography, history, and culture.

Lynne Larson. *Ghana.* Minneapolis: Lerner Classroom, 2010. Focuses on Ghanaian wildlife, people, and landscape, with information about the flag.

Bertha Vining Montgomery. *Cooking the West African Way.* Minneapolis: Lerner, 2010. A West African cookbook for kids.

Websites

Ghana Web (www.ghanaweb.com/). A website that gives information on all aspects of life in Ghana. The food link gives recipes. The information and facts link gives fast facts.

Oxfam, "Cool Planet" (www.oxfam.org.uk/coolplanet/kidsweb/world/ghana/index.htm). Run by a British charity, this website provides lots of information about Ghana's history, people, and geography. It includes a fact file.

National Geographic Kids, "Ghana" (http://kids. nationalgeographic.com/kids/places/find/ghana/). Facts, photos, and a map of Ghana.

Yahoo Kids, "Ghana" (http://kids.yahoo.com/ reference/world-factbook/country/gh--Ghana). Information about Ghana's people, government, economy, and issues facing the nation.

Index

Picture Credits

About the Author

Barbara Sheen is the author of more than 70 books for young people. She lives in New Mexico with her family. In her spare time, she likes to swim, walk, garden, and read. Of course, she loves to cook!